On Hal Moore

*"To his soldiers, he is Daniel Boone, Wild Bill
Hickok, James Bond, Teddy Roosevelt, and William
Tecumseh Sherman all rolled into six feet of bonehard
Kentuckian. Col. Moore is not only one of a handful
of occidentals always welcome at the inner sanctums
of the powerful Buddhist monks, but also to the envy
of many diplomats, he is on the same terms with the
christian leaders as well. Both spiritual groups say,
'He has won our understanding.'"*

Journalist, G.G. Burke, 1966

On Hal Moore

"To his soldiers, he is Daniel Boone, Wild Bill
Hickok, James Bond, Teddy Roosevelt, and William
Tecumseh Sherman all rolled into six feet of bonehard
Kentuckian. Col. Moore is not only one of a handful
of occidentals always welcome at the inner sanctums
of the powerful Buddhist monks, but also to the envy
of many diplomats, he is on the same terms with the
christian leaders as well. Both spiritual groups say,
'He has won our understanding.' "

Journalist, O.G. Burke, 1966

A General's Spiritual Journey

Lt. Gen. Hal G. Moore (Ret.)

Dedicated To: Julia Compton Moore

The Man: In Pursuit of a Deeper Understanding

The Servant Leader: The Monk Who Lives Within

The Spiritual Journey: "I always know He is there."

His Old Kentucky Home

Beloved West Point

Ia Drang – At Peace in War

Masher – One More Moore

The Book – For His Men

Face To Face With God

Lights – Camera – Action

"Julie, I'm Home"

Turning Points

A Just and Principled America

Living To Die – The Final Cut

The Final Resting Place

A National Treasure: Hal G. Moore

God's Command: Met With Costly Obedience

Son, If The "Helmet" Fits, Wear it: Passing The Torch

Unfinished Business: "Moore" To Do

Written by
Hal Moore's "Driver"

Hal Moore and the driver have agreed not to receive any compensation for this treatise.

October 1, 2007

Julia Compton Moore

Dedicated To: Julia Compton Moore (1929-2004)

After Julie's death, the Internet superhighway was full of the responses to her life. A few are shared.

"An extraordinary woman."
"I just cannot help but cry. What a wonderful woman she was. A silent partner doing heroic things of her own,"
"A lady who personified dignity, grace and charm."
"God bless Julia Moore. She was (& still is) an inspiration."
"What a trailblazer for all."
"She was a valiant SOLDIER!"

At her funeral on April 22, 2004, H. Gregory Moore (son), spoke these words... "Her gracefulness ensured that she could never turn away when she sensed others suffering. In this compassion, in this, was the breath of God. It fell closely on so many."

The Man: In Pursuit of a Deeper Understanding

"When we walk to the edge of all the light we have and take that step into the darkness of the unknown, we must believe that one or two things will happen ... There will be something solid to stand on, or we will be taught to fly." Anonymous quote.

Hal G. Moore has lived all of his life in pursuit of a deeper understanding. He speaks of the many occasions in his life where he has stepped into the darkness of the unknown.

He has always believed when in darkness there will be something solid to stand on, or he will be taught to fly.

It is difficult to understand the mystery of this man.

It should be clear that there is no intent to celebrate or bring undue emphasis to his journey. This is not about Hal Moore, as much as it is about the different journeys we all walk – and our learning from others along the way.

The public knows this hero for what he has achieved, and less what his spiritual journey has been.

He shares of moments and tells stories in his life.

It has been written that those who fail to tend to their inner stories risk creating a rift between what they believe and how they live.

Not so for Hal Moore.

His inner story has always been tended to. This man seems to always have felt God's presence in his soul.

On July 12, 2007, Hal Moore was asked, "Do you always feel God's presence in your life?' His answer in front of his daughter, Julie, was "No. We are in this life for temporal reasons, to do what we must do and what we are asked to do. I cannot imagine anyone *always* feeling God's presence in one's life – not even the most devout and religious. But, I always know that He is there." With that, Julie offered, "My father has always been a spiritual person."

Many over the years define him as a national treasure. If this be so, all the more reason for us to know the real Hal Moore, the man who spends more time on his knees than he does standing – and much time in prayer, spiritual study and reading.

On June 28, 2007, he was asked if this narrative could be written with his blessing. I shared the degree of spirituality that seemed to connect his life from childhood to today. His answer was, "If it will save one soul, let's do it!" On July 24, 2007, he stated, "There are only a few factual thoughts I wish to add, but I approve of the narrative if it might help another with their journey. We all need as much help as possible."

As I drive him from "here to eternity," he speaks of great things to change America – I call them Moore's "sermons on the mount."

On July 2, we drove to the hospital for back surgery. He spoke of his dear friend Joe Galloway and that Joe told him he was in the "business of words." I asked Gen. Moore, "What business are you in?" He pondered and stated, "I am in the business of eternity."

He is not the only one in deep pursuit of understanding. If the world wishes to model the best of its great leaders – Hal Moore is one to model.

The Servant Leader: The Monk Who Lives Within

From almost every angle, every setting, every occasion, the world sees three stars on each shoulder, even if they are not part of his attire for the day.

Certainly the obvious is fact. But there is another fact – a fact that this 85 year-old man goes from place to place in prayer and humility and grace.

There is a monk inside of Hal Moore, and the attire I see is that of a monk living a monastic type life. I close my eyes and imagine this man walking in prayer, head bowed and chanting softly. His head is shaved, leaving a band of hair below the ears, to symbolize the Crown of Thorns. His habit and sandals are all that he needs and wants.

It is then when I know that he has accepted the loving gaze of God.

In dealing with a life of grief – first his soldiers killed in battle, and now his wife – his screams are holy screams and only then, holy resignation.

His well-trained tongue is found not in speaking, but in silence.

To all of life, his responses are golden responses – in the golden years of his life.

Is the monk-like life for Hal Moore?

On August 4, 2007, in his sunroom, he stated, "Since Julie's death, I have considered becoming a monk. I have been to four retreats at the Abbey of Gethsemani in Kentucky, as it is only 25 miles from my birthplace. The first visit was right after graduation from West Point, as my roommate, James A. Herbert, and I attended a retreat before we reported for duty. Then I later went on my own. After reading *Seven Story Mountain* by Thomas Merton, I went once more, and met Merton. Merton is buried there."

I wonder what would have happened if Merton and Moore had looked into each other's eyes? Unfortunately, the two did not spend one-on-one time together.

As he has spent so much of his life sitting at the feet of the wise and his Lord, let us sit at the feet of this leadership sage whose spirituality speaks so true – and share his space and his thoughts.

The Spiritual Journey: "I always know He is there."

His Old Kentucky Home

"Bardstown, Kentucky is my birthplace, and it is where I grew up. My mother and father had four children. There was a strong spiritual influence from both of my parents.

"Dad went to mass at 6:00 AM every day, would return home, have breakfast with the family and then go off to work – the insurance business. I always remember my father leaving the house every morning to go to church.

"Mother was Methodist; however, she agreed to raise the children Catholic. She was more Catholic in some of her ways, as she would go to church and light candles for our family all of her life.

"1950 and 1951 were very tough years for our family. My brother, Bill, contracted polio in 1950 after his junior year at Notre Dame University; my father died suddenly at the age of 50 of a heart attack in June 1951 – and then I was shipped out to the Korean War in 1952 after Julie and I saw Bill graduate from Notre Dame walking the stage on crutches.

"My mother had the strength and love of God to lead our family for the next 50 years, without Dad. She and her God were a great team for the Moore family after Dad's death."

As Gen. Moore speaks of his family, one day spent driving spoke volumes of the spiritual aspect of his family.

We drove to Warm Springs, Ga. to the Roosevelt Rehabilitation Institute – the place where his brother, Bill, spent many months afflicted with polio. As we drove, Moore talked about the impact that polio had on the entire family. He believes that may have been the lead reason to his father's heart attack. "Bill's polio devastated Dad and Dad's death caused us all to hold on to what he held onto – his God."

"Julie and I were at Ft. Benning in late 1951, and we would drive over to visit Bill in his room."

When we arrived at the Institute, where do you think we went first on this campus of healing? We went to Bill's room; no longer one of the resident rooms. As we visited the wing and room, the past rushed back into Gen. Moore's mind.

At this moment, no words were spoken – not needed.

Later, Bill would come to walk again, with assistance, and Hal and family would come to know many better days.

A family's love?

The role of spirituality in a family?

Sooner or later there arises in every human heart the desire for holiness, spirituality – call it what you will. What Hal Moore picked up from his mother and father and siblings was a whole truckload of something very close to the heart – to the soul.

It is that "stuff" he is made of – from his old Kentucky home.

And his journey goes on!

Beloved West Point

Is it possible for there to be "love and a sense of stern, demanding authority combined at first sight?" To hear Hal Moore speak of that moment when he saw West Point for the very first time – it most definitely was an instant love and respect at first sight – never to fade away.

His years there are well documented and spoken by him as he writes and speaks on leadership. With every word, his love pours forth. Tears are often seen. What a love affair for 65 years this has been!

Through it all, the tough times and the good, a very special person stood in the wings of this leader to be, to listen, to counsel, to love and to pray for Hal Moore. He was always there for this man on a mission – on the grounds of his beloved West Point.

Monsignor George Murdock was his name.

In the very first year, Hal Moore sought solace, help and advice from "Padre" Murdock at the Holy Trinity Catholic Chapel.

Almost every day, during his West Point years, schedule permitting, Moore would go to daily Mass and visit Father Murdock. They would talk and pray together. Moore was even given odd jobs to perform at the chapel. A relationship was formed that became the foundation of Moore's spiritual journey to be. He was becoming a man, and more so, becoming a faithful servant – a servant leader.

Later in his young married years, a son was born. And he was given the name of – Murdock.

There was a moment of testing for Hal Moore near graduation from the Academy. He had many such moments, but this was different.

"Just before graduation week in 1945, the First Classmen of our cadet company had a meeting on a company picnic. During the meeting it was suggested that Cadet Ernest J. Davis, Jr., and his date and family not be invited to the picnic. I stood up and said that if Davis and his family and date were not invited that my date and parents and I would not attend. Quickly things were reversed and Davis and family attended with our other classmates and guests. Davis was one of three black cadets at West Point in the early 1940's and he was in the Cadet Company I was in."

This is shared as it shows in the smallest of ways the bigness of heart and leadership of Hal Moore in early years and his love of humanity – his spirituality.

In reflecting upon Gen. Moore's strong feelings about his spiritual growth at West Point, a book written by Morris Schaff, "The Spirit of Old West Point," tells it best. "The sensations of the new cadet when he reaches the Plain, lingers for a long while. There are two West Points – the actual West Point, and the overarching spiritual one, of which the cadet only becomes conscious when he graduates."

With Hal Moore, he has indeed been conscious a very long while.

And his journey goes on!

Ia Drang – At Peace in War

Ia Drang was the "valley of death." It was the very first major battle in Vietnam on November 1965. Lt. Col. Moore lost 79 men and the enemy lost over 1,000 killed and wounded. The battle became a book and the book became a movie.

God and the battlefield – how is it possible? How is it possible for a man, any man or woman to take his or her God to the battlefield, as if God chose one culture over another – one color over another – one nation over another?

We are a world of many differences and choices. Hal Moore has his God, and no doubt, He was very present in the midst of war and killing.

From others, it is said that Moore prayed over them, held soldiers

9

in their dying moments and carried some to the helicopters to place on the helicopter floor to be carried out – only to be placed later in body bags.

At peace in war? Yes. But what was that peace? Where did it come from? How did calm override crisis? Then and in many other moments in his life – a calm came over him.

One could attribute that peace to his training at West Point. If that were so, would not every cadet at the Academy walk out with the same "calm under fire" leadership style?

Simply, it was a gift given to him, unique to the way he looked at life and death, God or no God, and very quickly made decisions to act for his men, his country and his God.

Hal Moore was, before and after war, on a spiritual journey – and there is no reason to believe God was not in his life in battle either.

Recently I drove Gen. Moore to Ft. Benning and Columbus, Ga., as he shared much of his life with me that day. We saw the houses in which he and Julie once lived, visited his very first Battalion Headquarters Building on Kelly Hill, the location of the birth of one son, the Ft. Benning Headquarters and the National Infantry Museum, which displays Hal Moore and all that the battle, book and movie were about. When in the HQ, word traveled fast that Hal Moore was in the building. We were asked to visit the top floor. In doing so, Gen. Moore was met by senior officials and escorted down the hall – and shook hands with a long line of officers who met him along the way. At the end of the line, the commanding general took us into his office, and Hal Moore was given the highest degree of love and honor one could imagine. I was so proud for him! (Talk about flowers given to one before they die!)

When we left the building, I asked how was it that he was not killed in all of his battle moments and accidents. He just shook his head and stated, "One has no control over a bullet hitting you or another. You cannot think about it. If one comes out alive, as I have, one must live the rest of this life believing there is a reason that your life was spared and go forward to serve others. There will be a day when we all go 'out of the game.' One day I will be reunited with my men."

A leader he is.

In the 1990's, Moore revisited the Ia Drang battlefield, as he loves battlefields even to this day. On this visit, he met with the very leader who was trying to kill him back in 1965 – Lt. Gen. Nguyen Huu An, then Senior Lt. Col. It was a meeting of leaders who loved their country and their men - a meeting about many things, but what it was really about was forgiveness and becoming friends years later.

There is no question, based upon how they treated each other that spirituality in some form was present in the way Hal Moore received and visited with him – two warriors at peace in a very spiritual moment. If not, how was it in the very viewing case of Gen. An's important belongings was Moore's watch given to him

11

by Moore years earlier – a watch of ordinary means. Hal Moore visited the family after An died and, in surprise, saw the watch on display during the visit to pay respects.

Why? It was not about the value of a watch. It was about the value of life and what they really shared years later. Somehow Hal Moore touched that man's heart and soul – and the family knew it.

Speaking of heart and soul, I must share this story.

In June 2006, I was driving Gen. Moore and others to an old Civil War Battlefield outside Strasburg, Va. It was the site of the Battle of Cedar Creek, fought on October 19, 1864. Our reason for taking this route was it being a direct roadway to our meeting place. Moore's head did a 180-degree turn, as we stopped and listened to an account of the battle. Lt. Gen. Jubal Early took on Maj. Gen. Phil Sheridan, and it was as if Moore was locked into each word differently than the rest of us. He loved the warrior in Early, who had only one arm, leading his men against Sheridan. Moore identified with both generals - Sheridan, a West Point graduate in 1853 and Early, a West Point graduate in 1837. As we began to get into our vans to leave, I had to drag Gen. Moore away from the battlefield saying to him, "This is one battle that has already been fought and won – no need for Gen. Moore."

I wonder if Early or Sheridan had the gift of being at peace in war, as did Hal Moore?

When we returned to Moore's home a few days later, I walked

with him into his den for no special reason, and noticed a small painting on his wall in the corner. I had never really looked at it closely – it was Sheridan leading his men at Cedar Creek!!!

He could not explain, nor could I. This was just another unexplainable moment we have grown accustomed to.

History does prove the warriors that Early and Sheridan were. No less so for our Hal Moore.

In an article by G.G. Burke in January 1966, "Is He the 'Blood and Guts' General Patton We Need In Vietnam?" Burke's research and visits with Moore's soldiers produced revealing but not surprising responses.

"To his soldiers, he is Daniel Boone, Wild Bill Hickok, James Bond, Teddy Roosevelt, and William Tecumseh Sherman all rolled into six feet of bone-hard Kentuckian. The Vietnamese feel the same way. He is one of the few American officers who is greeted on the street with traditional Asian half-bow, from civilians as well as local officials and troops. Col. Moore is not only one of the handful of privileged occidentals always welcome at the inner sanctums of the powerful Buddhist monks, but also to the envy of many diplomats, he is on the same terms with the Christian leaders as well. Both spiritual groups say, 'He has won our understanding.' "

Gen. Moore was asked by Raymond Arroyo during his 2002 EWTN global interview, "Does your faith shape your leadership style?" His answer, "My faith in a future life has something to do with my leadership style. I am a strong believer in the promises Jesus Christ has made."

That's Hal Moore – direct and to the point.

And his journey goes on!

Masher – "One More Moore"

Very quickly, Hal Moore's new nickname became "one more Moore." He always wanted one more battle to fight. As they say, be careful what you pray for, you just might get it. Shortly after Ia Drang and LZ XRAY, Hal Moore was called upon to take on an even bigger battle at Bong Son.

It was called "Operation Masher." "One more Moore" got what he wanted and the Army had exactly the man they wanted to lead – once again.

Moore's brigade totaled 5,700 men. D-day arrived on January 28, 1966. After a week of combat, the 3rd brigade declared an end to the first phase. Americans had killed 603 by body count and estimated that an additional 755 had been killed as well. The brigade lost 77 Americans.

After three phases over six weeks, Col. Moore led his men in the killing of 1,342 enemy soldiers (with another 1,700 estimated killed), while losing 228 soldiers and 788 wounded.

In forty-one days of contact, Moore's brigade had clashed with

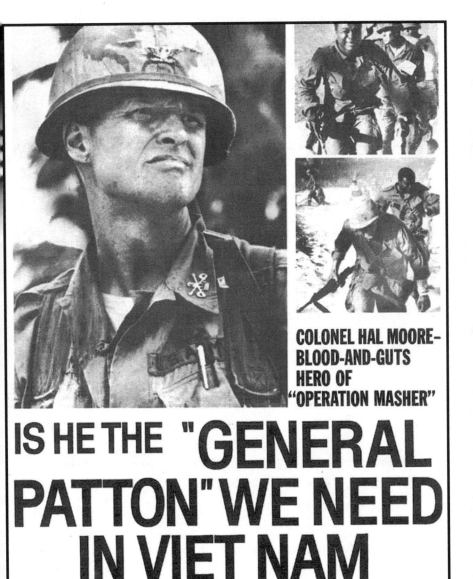

COLONEL HAL MOORE— BLOOD-AND-GUTS HERO OF "OPERATION MASHER"

IS HE THE "GENERAL PATTON" WE NEED IN VIET NAM

The above was found in the Hal Moore family archives.

all three regiments of the Sao Vang Division and claimed to have rendered five of nine enemy battalions ineffective for combat.

Moore had decided during Operation Masher that three Buddhist temples were not to be touched during battle.

It was here where Moore's reputation grew to be the American soldier who could find the Cong.

And his journey goes on!

The Book – For His Men

What can be said about a book that the world has read? The research and writing have been honored again and again. The co-authors experienced the story - up close and personal.

It is the "for his men" that is important in this treatise.

Hal Moore never did anything that was not for his men. Let us get this right.

In training, Hal Moore gave total self for his men. In war, Hal Moore gave total self for his men. In peace, Hal Moore has continued to give total self for his men.

It is why the battle became a book – for his men.

When home, he and Julie visited as many families as possible long after his men died. He needed to explain; he needed to help the family understand.

All of this for his men.

In the years just past, he travels and meets with anyone for his men.

It never was about a book. It was about honor and courage – and yes, his love for his men and his Julie.

Today, as he kneels in prayer, who do you suppose he prays for name by name – his men.

After the movie premiere at Ft. Benning, hundreds awaited Gen. Moore in the lobby. What was missed was Hal Moore quietly exiting the front entrance door into the night. I observed him pacing back and forth under a light in the parking lot. For ten minutes, he walked with hands behind his back, head bowed and in a special world all his own.

Then, I knew. He was in prayer – for his men.

After coming back to this life, he entered the door he had exited, walked into the lobby and joined the hundreds who awaited his presence. (Julie was in rare form – she was always in rare form.)

The book has achieved what he and Joe Galloway wished – to honor his men. Seventy-nine came home in boxes. To this day, he never forgets.

And until he dies, his life will continue to be – for his men and for his God.

And his journey goes on!

Face To Face With God

Somehow in life, Hal Moore knew that he would come face to face with God. He never knew when or how or why, but one day, he would feel and know God – face to face.

Considering his life, the exact moment could have been prayer, church, mountain settings, the births and marriages of his children, and travels around the world where he and Julie loved life so.

But no, God had other plans. He knew where and when and how he would present himself to Hal Moore.

As one might surmise, God's plan and timing were "heavenly."

In the 1990's when Hal and Joe and a few of the former soldiers returned to the battlefield with the national media, the stage was set for this Godly moment to come.

The crew had to spend the night, due to weather and Hal Moore's insistence. At midnight, Hal Moore's battlefield pilgrimage started. He had decided to walk the perimeter once more. He needed to do this in the worst way. He was being called, or better yet, summoned.

As he began his perimeter journey, the fighter in Hal Moore resurfaced. The soldier in him could smell the battlefield once more, he could hear the fighting and the screaming – as it all came rushing back. As much as he wanted to deny this fighter inside of him, in mind only, the warrior returned.

As he walked the perimeter, what kind of a fighter must Hal Moore have been 30 years earlier? Let us learn from one of his troopers.

From the words of a sergeant who fought with Moore when checking out an old Lao Valley cemetery, Moore yelled to him, "Put that helmet back on, trooper!" Then, Moore, a tall, rangy figure with silver eagles embroidered on his fatigue collars, a .357 Magnun clutched in his right hand, signaled to me, "Get down. Get down, man." He executed a perfect flying tackle, flooring me at the instant a sniper's bullet ricocheted off a gravestone in the cemetery. "Didn't you see that gleam in the trees?" Then another shot, and another. Moore stood up in full view. "Okay, guys," he ordered, "Let's get 'em." Leaping in front of us, Moore headed for a clump of trees in the middle of the burial ground, shooting as he dashed forward – sprinting from marker to marker in an exhibition of broken field running worthy of Cleveland's Jimmy Brown. We followed, shouting like Comanches, carbines blazing. By the time the evacuation helicopter arrived 57 minutes later, 22 Cong were dead or wounded, 11 captured. American casualties were slight and only one man was seriously wounded. It was a typical battle day for Col. Moore, the brigade commander the Saigon press calls, "the man who can find the Viet Cong." (This account was learned and written by G.G. Burke in January 1966.)

Yes, Col. Moore was indeed a fighter. In the year 2007, he told me in his sunroom, "The only place I have ever been comfortable was on a battlefield." I took issue with that statement. He then looked over at me with those steel eyes, and I knew then that his words were fact – not to be challenged.

With an overpowering love, as he continued his walk, his sense of war was overcome by a peace from above – from his God. Hal Moore was back and his higher power showed who was in control.

This night was written in the winds. Moore walked and prayed. His heart began to leap when his 79 dead soldiers were all trying to speak to him at once.

After walking the perimeter, he returned to the campsite. He looked up into the night, and underway was a shooting star display, unlike any other possible from this world.

Each shooting star was better than the last.
Each had the voice of one of his men.
Each man assured him that he was well.

The sky was afire, and it was then – that Hal Moore and God spoke – face to face. Moore felt loved and forgiven. Moore felt the long lasting guilt subside and die with the stars as they burned out in flight.

Whatever God said, this battlefield pilgrimage brought a peace within – a needed peace.

Closure was important for Hal Moore – for him to drive on.

Closure was important for God, as He had planned for just the right time to explain things to Moore.

Hal Moore needed to get on with his life without great guilt, and the bloody burden he had carried all those years.

Besides, something tells me that God told Hal Moore, "I am not finished with you yet."

If Hal Moore is right, and that he always knows when God is there, this "walk and talk with the stars" of a different kind is the truth we all seek in this life – the holiness we all wish to know before we die.

One of the men visiting the battlefield with Hal Moore in 1993 was Col. Tran Minh Hao, a soldier fighting to kill Moore in 1965. Hao wrote this poem after Moore's visit to the battlefield.

To remember the days of war!
We have come to you this afternoon.
Our old battlefield still here
Yet how to find your graves
Now hidden by thirty years of growth.
In your youth
Like leaves so green
Your blood soaks the earth red
For today's forest to grow
Words cannot describe how we miss you.

Our fingers trace the bark for clues of the days past
Imagining you resting for a thousand peaceful autumns
Feeling the loss of each of you.
We come to span a bridge
For the happiness of those living
On a calm autumn afternoon in Ia Drang
Veterans join hands
After thirty years, relive that battle
Between two sides of the frontlines
Time now we stand at each other's side remembering.
Generals and soldiers of years past
Bring back the months and years of history
Untroubled by ancient rifts
We look together towards the future
Hoping that generations to come will remember this deed.
Our peoples know love and bravery
We leave old hates for new friendships
Together we will live in peace
So that this land will remain ever green
Forever in peace and harmony.

And his journey goes on!

Lights, Camera, Action

As one moves from one scene in life to the next, we usually rely on our most important values when making decisions.

Hal Moore did!

When it became obvious that the best selling book would become a movie, Hal Moore and Joe Galloway met with numerous producers and directors who wanted to buy the rights to the book. The process was not a quick decision. As great things happen in Gen. Moore's life, Randall Wallace came calling. In their meeting, Hal Moore sensed something spiritual about Mr. Wallace and it was that spirituality that won out – the deal was made. Not because of the bottom-line, but because Hal Moore trusted and wanted Wallace's spirituality leading this project.

And if one has not seen the movie, there are scenes that show spirituality at work in the Moore family and on the battlefield.

Hal Moore was right.

Now, comes the tough part. Who would play Hal Moore? Randall Wallace had Mel Gibson in his hip pocket.

Moore flew to Los Angeles to meet with Mel Gibson. Shortly after they met, Mel asked Gen. Moore if he would join him at Mass. Later, Moore shared a favorite spiritual quote with Gibson. Halfway through the quote, Gibson finished it perfectly. Moore stood listening, as he was told by Gibson, "That very quote is on my locker in the studio."

"When Mel completed the quote, I was stunned." Shortly thereafter, Moore approved Gibson playing his life in the movie.

In jest, the only dissenting vote was Julie Moore, as she felt

Gibson was not as "good-looking" as her husband!!!

Since the movie, a close relationship remains between Gen.
Moore and Wallace, Gibson, Elliott, Stowe and the wonderful
cast. Often, out of the blue somewhere in the world Hal Moore
hears from his Hollywood friends. (Whatever is discussed stays
between the General and those from his days of "lights, camera,
action.")

On the 40th anniversary of the battle, it was Sunday morning,
November 11, 2005. Hundreds were at the Vietnam Wall in
DC honoring the dead from the battle. The sun began to rise,
as Amazing Grace was sung. Joe Galloway and Hal Moore
read the names of the dead. As I looked around to see the
unbelievable love being shared, I noticed Randall Wallace with
his arms around Hal Moore's two daughters – all three crying
their hearts out.

On the question of the emphasis on faith in the movie, Hal
Moore stated, "Randy Wallace knew of my standards and
principles and faith."

In his den, designed by Julie, are posters in five different
languages from the movie. It is a wall of disbelief; a wall that
only dreams are made of --- and this dream came true! To know
Hal Moore, one would never know what life he has lived.

Why? The answer lies in the quote that he and Mel Gibson share
in common!

"Discover to me, O My God, the nothingness of this world, the greatness of heaven, the shortness of time, and the length of eternity." Pope Clement XI

Yes, Hal Moore got it right – Wallace and Gibson were a great team and the decisions made were not about "show me the money." With Hal Moore, decisions are about "show me your soul."

What did Gibson do to accurately portray Moore? "(He) really gave me every aspect of his experience which came naturally as we hung out for long enough. We visited every single grave of the boys that died and he would tell me all of this stuff about all these guys, talking about each one for a while before going on to the next one."

"My father and Hal Moore were the same kind of guy, you know? He's a WWII veteran and they have the same religious beliefs." Gibson asked his father how he prepared for battle. "He had these particular prayers that you have on your person that are supposed to protect you from being hit and in fact guarantee victory. My dad carried the same prayer as Hal Moore, and I don't know a lot of people who do that." (Now on Gibson's locker!)

On Friday, March 1, 2002, a Washington Post story about the movie, written by Stephen Hunter states, "… If ever a man were born to command a battle, it was Hal Moore. Photos of the real man reveal something Gibson tries hard to convey but cannot quite: a pugnacious aggression, a bulldog's ferocious

25

countenance. But he's no tyrant. He believed in unit as family, in respect running up and down the ranks, in love rather than fear. Odd, isn't it – one of the things you need to prevail on a bloody field is love, which turns out to be more tactically useful by far than hate."

On Hal Moore, Gibson has stated, "He had like a shield around him. General Moore is a man of great faith who believes in something greater than himself."

And if you know the spiritual journey Gen. Moore is traveling, surely you must also know that he prays every day for his Hollywood friends.

Mel was right – there is a shield around Hal Moore.

And his journey goes on!

"Julie, I'm Home"

As great losses do to all of us, we are reduced to a "nothingness" that darkens our journey. Where do we turn and to whom?

Thankfully, those in our lives show up and love on us in surprising ways – ways that give us hope in our grief.

Allow me to explain.

One early morning, not long after Julie died, I placed in Gen. Moore's mailbox a letter for him to read. The letter dealt with my feelings that Julie had to go first – it was meant to be. Not knowing whether the letter reached him or if read at all, I just hoped it might help in some small way.

The very same day, Gen. Moore called and asked if I might drive him to the local Auburn airport, wait and then return him to his home. I asked no questions and responded as asked. He made no mention of my earlier letter.

When we arrived, a jet was standing off the runway near the terminal. Hal Moore got out, walked up the stairs and the door closed behind him.

It was none of my business what was going on, or who was inside. Not sure how long I waited, but some 30 minutes or so later, the door opened and Gen. Moore stepped out and down the steps. He walked over, got in, and we drove back to his home.

He thanked me, and no other words were spoken. One thing was different, however, he carried a small piece of paper with him that was not taken onto the plane. Upon arriving at his home, he got out, waved and that was it.

Into the evening, he called and asked if I might join him at home. When I arrived, he sat with the paper. He explained, "A copy of one page was given to me by a friend. He noticed a truth I needed to know. It clearly spelled out for me why Julie had to go before me - which she needed to be spared the grief of my going first. I would not have wanted that. This was contrary to the way I had planned things. I was always to go first. What is so compelling is that this paper I was given says exactly what your letter stated this morning. I now know that she had to go first – no question."

I looked at the small one page, and I heard a deep sigh from Gen. Moore, as if 1,000 pounds had been lifted off of his shoulders. He had just learned an insight that had never occurred to him and it was this messenger from afar who struck gold with his great gift of time and words.

I never learned who was inside that jet – for it really does not matter, other than they must love him very much.

Our drives do not begin or stop here.

One evening some 18 months ago, Gen. Moore and I were driving back from a visit at Ft. Benning, Georgia. As we drove into the night, neither spoke – the silence was too good. Then he stated, "It will be dark by the time we get home." I gave no response (I have learned that is best with him, as he wanted no response.)

After a few miles, he stated, "When Julie was alive, when I would come home, the lights would be on and the music would be playing for me. I would be so thankful to enter the home she made so warm and loving. As I would enter the door, I would yell so that she could hear, 'Julie, I'm home!'

Once more, with a heavy heart, I just lowered my head, said nothing and continued our drive home to his dark and cold house.

And then, in his soft emotional manner, these words were spoken, "When I know that I will be coming home after dark, I now turn on the lights before I leave and turn on the music, so that when I return, it will be as if she were home – waiting like the 54 years of our marriage."

I said nothing, as we began to reach Auburn, Alabama.

Finally, from the lips that had kissed Julie's all their years, the truth of their love and the reason for his grief, poured forth. Only the engine could be heard, when he shared, "Know what I do now upon entering our home? I still yell – 'Julie, I'm home – knowing there is no Julie to run to – to hug – and to thank God for."

No response needed, as the tears flowed. I stared ahead, turned right, turned left – and we were in his driveway. No words were spoken. The house lights were off, no music was to be heard, and no Julie waiting for this man in his grief, two years after she had died.

We parted, and he walked up the stairs to the deck. I wanted to wait. I wanted to hear his yell to his soul mate, "Julie, I'm home." But I knew better. That was a God thing. That was about a love between two lovers who had become one over the past 54 years.

My God, how does one go on?

How does one even begin to live for the next day?

What does one live for?

In all that I have heard from Hal Moore in his years of grief as we drive the roads, it has been his prayer time, his church, his readings, his crying, his spirituality that has given him reason to carry on – to make it through one more day.

At his choice, he chooses to stay in their home.

It is Julie's spirit that he will never ever leave. Photographs are turned over and found down the hall when he comes home. In a dead sleep, he bolts to a sitting position in bed, to find Julie standing in the doorway for a few seconds – and then she disappears back into the heavens.

They talk. They love still. She is there for him in different ways – but her presence is alive and well.

The General sees to that.

To best understand this man's spirituality and journey through grief – if one ever gets through it – please ponder every word from his July 12, 2007 note to a man he has never met, who lost his wife to cancer on July 10, 2007 – two days earlier.

On three-star letterhead, he deals with his grief by being there for another in their grief.

"Dear John,

I have been told of your recent loss of your wife, and asked
to give the enclosed to you. I know that all close losses are
different because of the various relationships. I lost my precious
wife, Julie, - of 54 years – in 18 April '04 after a two-month bout
with cancer. I have received some comfort from almost daily
attendance at Church services – or visits to the Chapel to pray. I
also have come to accept that her death was the will of God, and
that's tough to accept, but for peace of mind. I must accept it
and pray for our reunion in a far better place. I have been asked
to give you the enclosed book titles, which have helped me. I
hope they help you. Sooner or later we shall all be re-joined -
forever – in a far better place. In Christ, signed (Hal Moore)"

Attached note: "Here are the titles of 2 books which, among
several, were/are very helpful to me. 'Heaven' by Randy Alcorn
(Tyndale) and 'Seven Choices – Finding Daylight after Loss
Shatters Your World' by Elizabeth Harper Neeld (Warner Books).
Signed (Hal Moore)"

From "Julie, I'm home," to a "far better place," the loss of his
soul mate and spiritual journey is a battle of the worst kind – a
battle where there is no enemy to defeat – to kill.

For this warrior, his life on this earth is a day-to-day battle with
the enemy within. Like all other previous wars, he has a plan
and is working at following God's will.

There are those who love him so, who wish for him to move to
another home, another state – to be nearer his children. There

would appear to be many practical reasons for such a case to be made.

However, in all the years of love, cases to be made "for the practical" seldom win.

And who knows, Julie standing in his doorway in the middle of the night just may be far more real than any of us will ever know.

And his journey goes on!

Turning Points

Gen. Moore believes that all of us have turning points in our lives.

Let us read the very words of Hal Moore, as he speaks and writes about turning points in 2006.

"I believe we all have turning points in our lives that can change the course of a life and one's beliefs forever.

In my case, November 14-16, 1965 changed my life forever. After 18 months of preparation at Fort Benning, Georgia, I and my men, the 1st Battalion, 7th Cavalry, were ordered into Ia Drang Valley, South Vietnam to fight the first major battle of the war. With 450 men, we were dropped by helicopter into a small clearing, Landing Zone (LZ) X-RAY, and were immediately surrounded by 2,000 North Vietnamese soldiers. The next three days became a valley of death. After three days of face to face combat, the enemy lost – killed and wounded more than 1,000 men – and 79 of our soldiers lost their lives.

One of those men was Sgt. Jack Gell. Holding him in my arms as he died, and seeing other soldiers go down changes a person. Ask any soldier who fought for his or her country – they know. You are never the same.

Sgt. Gell is buried next to my wife at Ft. Benning and I, too, will be buried there. For years, my wife and I attempted to reserve the grave site next to Sgt. Gell, but it was already reserved. Three days before Julie died in April 2004, we were notified that it was "available." Mrs. Gell and her children released it for us, as she had planned to be buried there. Now, one day, I will be buried with my wife and my men – what a way to go out!

From that turning point in my life, I have lived driven for an even greater purpose than before and one was to later tell America about these great men – which was done in a book and movie.

What would our young people have become, all of them, if they had been able to serve their country by their lives, instead of their deaths?

From that very turning point in 1965, I knew then that I wanted to continue living for a better America. My beliefs became my road map for living. Today, at 85 years, I can connect what I believe, what I have done with my life, and what I am doing with that "turning point."

There have been other turning points, such as the loss of my wife, Julie. Grief of any kind is so difficult to live through. All of us grieve in different ways and working through it is hard for us all.

Our youth in America have turning points – more than they know, and many of their choices may develop them into better leaders in the future. As I think about America and our young persons, our future lies in their hands and the turning points in their lives.

I pray they understand the value of such moments in their precious lives.

However, they cannot achieve this alone. All of us who have walked before them must provide ways for them to grow their character and their values.

We must impress upon them the need for trust in all relationships, as it is here where leaders are most effective.

Falling and failing are a part of life, and if those moments are turning points, one can get back up and try again.

In life, three strikes and you are not out!

I wish to conclude with what I believe more than all else in life: I believe in God the Almighty and His hand in the turning points in our lives!"

There are few ways to better reflect upon the turning points in our lives and how we might learn from them.

Study of General Moore's writings confirms a consistent spiritual aspect to his leadership teachings, for all ages.

And his journey goes on!

A *Just and Principled America*

As Gen. Moore dealt with his grief after Julie passed away, on April 18, 2004, I received a call from Maj. Gen. Peter Boylan, President of Georgia Military College. He asked if I might meet him for lunch soon in Columbus, Ga.

A week later, lunch turned into a three-hour discussion on matters of a just and principled America and the ethics and character of youth – and that of Hal Moore. At the very center of our discussions were Hal and Julie Moore. The intent was to honor both in the years to come through this "institution to be," but there was an even deeper intent. General Boylan stated, "We all must help to redirect his grief. He must have purpose and a goal to get through this life without Julie."

That was it. Redirect. Purpose. We all must help.

Gen. Boylan had a plan and several others who believed in Gen. Moore and his philosophy and values and teachings on leadership had a plan.

These plans and vision became the true beginning of The National Endowment for The Public Trust.

After two months of dealing with his and America's loss, Gen. Moore was asked if he would allow this "institution in the making" to embrace his life and that of his Julie, to become our cornerstone and would he be the founder.

Would he found a great leadership institution, to be based on his spirituality and sense of right and justice? Would he?

After much prayer and many weeks, Gen. Moore stated, "I believe that America needs this, and I believe this is very important. I will be the founder because I do know leadership from top to bottom, and I do know that we can make a difference.

"I will lead and I will do what I can as long as I am able."

That was in June 2004.

On August 10, 2004, Gen. Hal Moore was the very first person to affix his name to the Declaration for a Just & Principled America – the very document that has become the foundation of The Public Trust.

From that day forward, The Public Trust has listened to, and is learning from its founder. His every breath, his counsel and his actions are bold spiritually. He speaks up and offers wisdom that comes from above. Not that he is alone, but that the vision to advance public trust must be grounded in the way we treat and love one another.

Hal Moore loves.

The President of The Public Trust, Rear Adm. Paul Rosser, is quoted on film, "We must learn to love each other more."

Are Rosser and Moore in lockstep?

As the plans grew for this institution, daily and weekly reports were presented to Moore. Meetings were held all over America and Hal Moore was not only there, but demanded that the ball be moved. Action!

And as unplanned events happened, Gen. Moore would say, "That is Divine Providence at work."

With each progress report, Gen. Moore would frame the result or status with his view of humanity and life – a spiritual perspective.

In meetings, his presence lowered voices in rooms and raised the level of respect and civility in the room. It is who he is, and it is this leadership style that The Public Trust has worked so hard to engrave in the souls of all who wish to give birth to this cause, so sought after.

America's youth is one of the programming priorities.

Gen. Moore's passion is to speak on leadership, especially to America's youth. He was asked to speak to teenage boys on leadership, and I was his driver on this day. Other program speakers included, Dr. Kevin Ryan, Maj. Gen. Lou Hennies and Maj. Gen. Peter Boylan. These four men have one thing in common – each has lived their lives for the character development of young people. Each spoke the most powerful of truths and offered counsel to these boys and their parents.

When Hal Moore spoke, he paid respects to those men with him that evening who have devoted their lives to the character of others. No doubt, each has the greatest of achievements in changing the lives of others.

The final words spoken to the audience by Moore were these, "Young men, what lies within each of you is the greatest of leadership potential. Never forget that it is your being in touch with your spirituality that will serve you best in the leadership dreams you may have."

As we drove home, all was quiet. No words were needed. He had said it all.

The next morning in church in Auburn, Al., Boylan, Moore and Ryan could be seen kneeling in prayer together, and later the three were interviewed for a newspaper front-page article on the character of America's youth.

With each turn in the road, a new idea often comes forth from Gen. Moore's thinking and is soon to be on the agenda for consideration.

On one fine day as Gen. Moore was picked up from the Atlanta airport after another one of his leadership speeches, we drove south on I-85 toward "War Eagle" country to Auburn, Al. once more. When we drive, our minds tend to fly with opportunities and reasons for The Public Trust to help others.

On this occasion, I asked him if he had ever heard of a National

Leadership Day, Week, or Month in America. The answer was "No." We drove several miles without words and then he asked, "What about trust rather than leadership? He then pulled out a piece of paper and started scribbling. He drew a diagram and began to explain his trust triangle, which soon became a circle, which soon became a "roundtable" as we spoke. He explained and as he did so, I realized that what happens at a roundtable with persons is a sharing more intimate and more loving than not. Hal Moore then stated, "This is the way Jesus led others, in a circle of trust." It was then that the "roundtable approach" was planted – to eventually lead to the Servant Leadership & Management Roundtable for The Public Trust.

As with many developments of this institution, there appears to be a Divine Nature to the many unplanned and unexplained events.

One very specific event occurred when Gen. Moore spoke outside of Vail, Colorado at the request of Pat McConathy in the winter of 2006. He spoke to more than 100 men at the Yarmony Creek Ranch. What has happened since is a string of amazing events, equally viewed by McConathy and Moore as being Divine.

Since lunch with Gen. Boylan in 2004, it is safe to say that Moore's grief has been redirected. A redirection team has been at work to do so – from Joe Galloway and their second book, from Dick Strong and his Vail winter meetings, to The Public Trust – Hal Moore has given birth to an educational institution to advance public trust in America.

When Gen. Boylan and I speak and continue our pursuits, he just smiles. He knows and I know. Others will soon know. Hal Moore's grief has been redirected – never to go away – but with purpose, he lives without his Julie.

Moore calls it Divine Providence. Who are we to disagree?

Since August 10, 2004, more than 100 founding fellows have affixed their signatures to the Declaration from every part of America. It is a body of men and women, led by Hal Moore, who wish to advance and celebrate public trust.

We drive and we drive.

And his journey goes on!

Living To Die - The Final Cut

How most unusual it is to witness one who is living and working at dying – a death in this life – so that his eternal life will be spent with his God, his Julie and family – and his men!

Almost daily, there is great evidence as to this aspect of his journey to make the "final cut," as he speaks of it. From his days of knowing that only the best at something makes the "final cut" – makes the team, makes the journey – he views Judgment Day to be just that.

He has never been one who believed one earned his way into the next life, but as he also says, "I believe in stacking the deck."

As we are all apt to do, we grab onto the spoken word of another. We listen and then we act or react. The spoken or written word is about how to build relationships and live our lives.

In the case of Hal Moore, no spoken words are necessary. Just following in his footsteps on any given day is convincing enough.

All of his correspondence includes references to spirituality, to include how he often signs books and photographs for others.

The books he reads come from the family of the Divine.

The prayers he prays come from the most holy of places.

When he greets another, his eyes see and communicate a true sense of caring and compassion.

His one-hour daily visits to the Chapel of his church are for his Julie, family and men. And this does not include his almost daily Mass participation at another time of the day.

The three by five cards he carries in his pocket and his reading materials are most often reminders – to pray for this or that person.

In a drive to Tuskegee, Alabama to the Veterans' Hospital, we spoke of eternity – his strong will to make the "final cut." As we came upon the beautiful historical campus of Booker Washington and George Carver, Tuskegee University, he stated, "There is nothing more important for all of us than to make the 'final cut."

I shared with him my knowledge of the spirituality of Washington and Carver and how they worked to influence youth in that way. Every Sunday night, Washington would deliver an address to his students about faith, character and right. When Carver would take his students into the fields of Alabama, he spoke of the flower and the peanut as gifts from God – and his mother earth - his laboratory. There was indeed a great sense of spirituality in both these great leaders in a different time in history.

Today, Hal Moore lives in the same way.

Two years ago, on a flight to Milwaukee, we sat next to one another. We both pulled out our reading material. His reading was on "Purgatory." As he read, I listened to his offerings and observations. For two hours Hal Moore shared his views on Purgatory – a place where one does not make the "final cut" – initially. A holding pattern it is!

It occurred to me that this man next to me was different – very different from most persons I have ever known.

As he spoke, I thanked God for the privilege to be in his presence at all, at this moment – even to being his "driver" when possible.

We then later flew to Vail for a meeting of some 20 others for three plus days. It was at this meeting that I observed the way others treated and visited with Gen. Moore. They too knew that he was very different – even those who were meeting him for the very first time.

The difference was and is – Hal Moore breathes every breath to make the "final cut" and it is that difference that others are drawn to. To this man, salvation is not an event; it is a process. There is a sense that if anyone can explain Heaven not having been there, this man just might come very close to getting it right.

And his journey goes on!

The Final Resting Place

It was April 18, 2007. A very special day – the third anniversary of Julie's death.

It was my privilege to drive Gen. Moore to the Ft. Benning Cemetery and to visit the dead – his men, his in-laws and his Julie.

We have made this journey three times now.

This time one thing was different. Without his consent, my camera was in hand, knowing with his being hearing challenged, he would not hear the click of photos being taken.

In route, we stopped to pick up flower arrangements for his family.

As we drove into the cemetery and parked, he gathered the

arrangements, and we started to walk. As I do, I stayed away, far behind this man of men.

He led, and I followed.

All was quiet in the cemetery. The headstones were lined up left and right for the eye to see. The wind blew, and the sun was shining. The clouds above were moving at a fast clip.

Our first stop was the grave of his mother and father-in-law, Col. and Mrs. Compton. He fell to his knees and began to work the arrangement so that it would fit perfectly in the provided holder. After the flowers were tall and straight, his arm went out to them – to the headstone – and he prayed.

We then traveled to the headstone that read "Julia Compton Moore."

He dropped to his knees and performed surgery on the arrangement as before. After several minutes, he was satisfied with the presentation. He then began praying, holding on to the stone with every breath and possible strength he could draw upon. It was as if he were drawing strength from her – again.

Standing far from him, I just observed this life kneeling. He prayed and he prayed and he prayed. At that time, I began to "click" away. This moment had to be forever. (See photo)

God, he loves her so and it was his God who played the music as he danced on his knees with his beloved. I turned away – I could not watch this dance of love.

He rose and turned to me, motioning me over to him.

We then walked the rows of every fallen soldier under his leadership in 1965, stopped, knelt and prayed. I listened to his stories, how they died and how young they were. He held this one in his arms as he died, he carried that one back into the helicopter after he died, and he heard once more the screams of young men calling for their Moms.

Three hours or so later, another Hal Moore lesson had been put into practice.

This leader never stops loving – never.

En route home, no words were spoken. A surprise and unplanned call from Bo Callaway occurred. This former Secretary of the Army had approved Gen. Moore's third star in 1974. I handed the phone to Gen. Moore, and they spoke. Mr. Callaway was returning my call to confirm a future meeting, not knowing the day or that Hal Moore would be with me. I sensed a great love and respect between the two. Hal Moore was very moved to have spoken to his dear old friend of many years – on that day.

Did it just happen or was there Divine Providence as to the exact timing of that call? There is no doubt in the General's mind!

On our ride home I shared with Gen. Moore that I had taken

photos of our day and would show them to him for approval. One day later, he looked at each one and nodded.

As we continued our journey, he stated, "I will be with my Julie one day and that will be our final resting place together."

It must be said. Whatever spirituality Hal Moore has, the true source of that holiness does not come from God only. What he was, and what he has become, and how he believes was not handed to him directly by his God.

God chose Julie to be His messenger of spirituality and it is because of her that he is the complete man that he is. Perhaps the lesson here for all of us is just this – that God works through humanity to teach and to love. He is not only in the heavens above but also in the hearts of those He sends to us.

Julie once received a note from a young friend, "You have taught me how to live my life. How I want to affect people. How I want to support them. How I want to be in love with my husband. How I want to spread a love for life."

Julia Compton Moore had taught Hal Moore well, but the list of those who learned from Julie is long indeed.

There was nothing to say, just drive on driving on.

Fortunately, Hal Moore's spiritual journey goes on still!!!

A National Treasure: Hal G. Moore

It may appear rather bold to suggest that a man could be considered a national treasure. As the years have brought many into Gen. Moore's life, it has been heard once if not hundreds of times from the lips of others – Hal Moore is a national treasure.

Each time that is said, I wonder. This term I have never used about him, largely because that should be reserved for the obvious and clear-cut treasure of a nation or at least I thought.

"The idea of national treasure, like national epics and national anthems, is part of the Romantic nationalism. Nationalism is an ideology, which supports the nation as the fundamental unit of human social life, which includes shared language, values and culture. Thus national treasure, part of the ideology of nationalism is shared culture. It can be a shared cultural asset or may refer to a rare cultural object. There are thousands of national treasures around the world. Many are often people." (Wikipedia)

To err on the side of being conservative regarding applying the term national treasure to Hal Moore, let us consider the life of Hal Moore.

. Since 1945, he has devoted sixty-three (63) years to leading others and the teaching of leadership in America to thousands of men and women.

. In 1965, at LZ XRAY in Vietnam, he lost 79 men – in a battle against more than 2,000 enemy over a three-day period. It was a miracle that he and all of his men were not slaughtered. At the end of the battle, the enemy retreated having lost more than 1,000 of their soldiers killed or wounded.

. His very first book became a New York Times Best Seller, which led to it becoming a movie featuring Mel Gibson as Hal Moore.

. There are second and third books underway, to be published in the coming months.

There just is no stopping Hal "Eveready" Moore.

This is the very public life of Hal Moore. The world seeks him out to autograph at every chance.

America has few heroes left, who qualify for such an honor. And honor is what this man has been and is all about.

With this said, it is the very private life of Hal Moore that truly qualifies him for being considered a national treasure. Those who know him best have no doubt.

Perhaps this moment will offer increased clarity on national treasures – particularly when one national treasure may be speaking about another.

In a meeting in Washington DC with Ambassador Dr. David Abshire, former Ambassador to NATO, personal advisor to

President Ronald Reagan, and current President of The Center for the Study of the Presidency, it was Dr. Abshire who spoke of Hal Moore, "He has always been my hero and is a national treasure." I telephoned Gen. Moore in front of Dr. Abshire and they spoke for 5 minutes with joy and excitement – one national treasure to another – both champions for a just and principled America.

In 2006, I observed a similar event of sharing in Gen. Moore's home. No driving required. Ambassador Andrew Young, another national treasure, stopped by to visit and share their mutual respect for each other's contributions to America. Dr. Young was in Auburn to speak and Gen. Moore was there to listen. When they connected, the internal soul of America shifted, if ever so slightly. That is what happens when two or more national treasures come together for the good of others.

As they spoke, it was very clear just how important it is for America's great leaders to have important dialogue and share their mutual love of our nation – particularly those who qualify as national treasures.

When Hal Moore "goes out of the game," let America try to replace him. The same goes for Abshire and Young.

Ralph Waldo Emerson writes it so beautifully. *"It is natural to believe in great men. The search after a great man is the dream of youth and the most serious occupation of manhood. Other men are lenses through which we read our own minds. The great are near; we know them at sight. They satisfy expectation and fall into place. When nature removes a great man, people explore the horizon for a successor, but none comes, and none will. His class is extinguished with him."*

If we are to apply the writing of Emerson to the de nition of a national treasure, Hal Moore's class will be extinguished with him. No need to seek a successor. None will come – ever.

Yes, we know them at sight and he is right under our very nose. And as opposed to his death announcement declaring him a national treasure, let us bestow such an honor on this "man of honor" while he is still alive and well.

A National Treasure - Hal G. Moore.

God's Command: Met With Costly Obedience

Gen. Moore heard the command of God early on, and that command was met with costly obedience. For, Moore always obeys commands from "above."

Sometime in Hal Moore's life there was a secret turning of his face towards God, a personal and wholly tranquil "choice" of his soul for his Master and Savior.

Over these most recent of years, as Gen. Moore enters the lives of others, statements are made that speak to his spiritual journey. One such statement was from Paul Rosser, "He is the most pure human I have ever met." Another was from John Sykes. In sitting next to him after having known Hal Moore for three days at a small gathering, John shared, "What is going on here?" (He knew what was going on!) Also, it was John's question that actually started this narrative. Jim Volker stood with me and watched Gen. Moore after having heard him speak, "There is something about him that I wish to know better." These examples are but small snapshots of how Hal Moore impacts others in this life.

It is as if he sees the foretaste of Heaven and breathes an atmosphere of familiar and dear. With each breath, what could be so dear you may ask?

The perfume of his Julie!

This spiritual journey for Hal Moore - the man, the servant leader, and the general - has not been walked without years of weariness and heartache battled and overcome, by a steadfast, unflinching desire to conquer self. As he has lived, a spiritual way was acquired, one day at a time.

Hal Moore does not "see to believe;" he "believes to see."

Recently in DC for meetings, I stopped my car near the Vietnam Wall. When I approached panel 3 East, where the names of his soldiers are engraved, I read over each name. As my fingers touched the names, I called Hal Moore on my cell phone and told him what I was doing. I read the name of one – he said nothing – and then he repeated the name. I read another and he repeated it. With his voice on one end of the line and my fingers on the other end, there was no doubt that he and his men were connecting in some far off way that I do not understand.

May we all learn something from Hal G. Moore's journey. From the beginning of his life to today, there has been one common thread – his spirituality. It all began in Kentucky as a boy, through his days at West Point, on to the battlefields, and into a life of speaking, writing a book and then – the movie. The loss of Julie changed his life. But with each turning point, he relied on one thing – his faith and the evermore pursuit of a deeper understanding.

There is no greater evidence of love, than a family's love. Since Gen. Moore's successful back surgery on July 2, 2007, his children have poured on all the love possible, taking turns to be his caregiver and all that entails. Before surgery, he was unsure of their availability. One month later, he is very sure of one thing – how much his children love their father.

Something tells me, with the glances his children have been giving him and his returning them with a smile and no words – "I love you" is being spoken with every look.

Son, If The "Helmet" Fits, Wear It: Passing The Torch

In April 2007, a young West Point cadet visited Gen. Moore two months prior to graduation. Moore finished in 1945 and Sam Ketcham graduated in 2007. The conversation was joyful and open. After walking into Gen. Moore's office and den, all was quiet. On the shelf was Lt. Col. Moore's helmet worn in battle. Moore handed the helmet to young Sam and invited him to put it on. Sam hesitated, and with great caution, finally did so. At that very moment, as photos were being taken, tears flowed from young Sam. Moore stated, "Son, if the helmet fits, wear it." The words were a Hal Moore challenge to the cadet. The moment was symbolic. The torch was being passed to Sam – and to many other young men and women who will follow in the footsteps of our nation's national treasures.

Gen. Moore later autographed the photo to Sam for graduation with this inscription – "Seek the will of God and never quit!"

Unfinished Business: "Moore" To Do

With regard to what he believes, that "God is not finished with him yet," he continues to love on others.

As Hal Moore continues his life of servant leadership, the degree of unfinished business has no boundaries. An opportunity to reach 70,000 American soldiers at war was offered by "Operation Gratitude" – a truly remarkable organization in Southern California, which functions as a preparer and deliverer of care packages to soldiers in Iraq and Afghanistan. In December 2007, the care packages will include "A General's Spiritual Journey." Carolyn Blashek, founder, stated "General Moore's message will be powerfully felt by all troops, regardless of their spirituality. We are privileged to include his treatise."

Hal Moore had back surgery on July 2.

On August 15, 2007, Hal Moore traveled to Colorado to meet

recent veteran soldiers who have returned home alive, but without all their body parts.

Many cannot walk.
Many cannot hug.
Many can hardly think of their futures.

Gen. Moore is going to honor and pray for those soldiers!!! They may not be his men, but they are men and women who have paid a deep price to serve our nation.

Regardless his pain and recovery from surgery, Hal Moore always is where he is needed most.

Once there, Hal Moore found "one more thing he can do." There was unfinished business. He walked away with every soldier's name, with each to be placed on his prayer cards and to pray for them every day – for their lives and their making the "final cut."

Moore reached down and visited with each soldier. With each, fresh tears could be seen. The words were soft but the hugs were hard. Observation could not reveal who helped whom the most!

Moore's last hours spent at the Yarmony Creek Ranch were truly memorable, as a six o'clock sunrise greeted him on top of a small summit. As the group shared breakfast and spoke of their most meaningful experience the last three days, it was time with the wounded veterans that captured their hearts.

But the sunrise and power of the moment took the breath away from the visitors.

The world stopped – or so it seemed. The last to speak was Gen. Moore.

"As I look upon these plains and mountains, the beautiful sunrise, I see yesterday. I see buffalo roaming the plains and the Indians with their tee-pees tucked away in the valley. I see an eagle or two flying the skies. I see life hundreds of years ago and now – they are gone and we are here. They are dust and soon shall we be dust. What I see here is the temporary nature of all life. All of life is so transitory. As we embrace this God moment, part of us may think we will be here forever. I will leave these mountains and this valley knowing that I will soon be with the buffalo and the Indians of years past. So will you. Others will soon stand where we stand. May we know the 'nothingness of this world, the greatness of heaven, the shortness of time, and the length of eternity.' "

Yes, the world had stopped. With eyes closed and heads lowered, the seven men walked away – perhaps better men and more in touch with their higher power.

And as I drove him to the airport, his words were, "There is still unfinished business to do. Drive on."

And driving on we will!

Special Note: *With Hal Moore's private spiritual journey shared, he is inviting all of us to step out of darkness with him, knowing that there is solid ground under foot, or that we will be taught to y. Gen. Moore has approved this narrative, not because he believes he is any more worthy than any one else. In fact, to allow this most private part of his life to be in print at all, is due to his love of humanity and it possibly saving one more soul. It is with that intent that "A General's Spiritual Journey" has been shared. The driver and his wife are friends and neighbors. He and his wife, with many others in America, enjoy the privilege of being there for Gen. Moore in his golden years. Special thanks to the children of Julie and Hal Moore for their support and love of this work. We are most unworthy and deeply priviledged to put into writing Hal Moore's spiritual journey. Char and Toby*

At 68 years old, Hal Moore stands at 12,000 feet, having climbed a mountain in Russia with twenty other men half his age. After leading the group to the top of the mountain, former Russian soldiers making the climb with him volunteered to serve under Moore should he ever "assume another command!"

On Tuesday, September 25, 2007, St. Louis Cardinals Manager Tony La Russa (left) and star player Albert Pujols (right) join Hal Moore at dinner after the Milwaukee Brewers game in Milwaukee at Mo's Restaurant.

Gen. Moore and Julia at Hollywood Premiere of "We Were Soldiers" in 2002.

*"Discover to me, O my God, the nothingness
of this world, the greatness of heaven,
the shortness of time, and the length of eternity."*
Universal Prayer of Clement XI

"Discover to me, O my God, the nothingness
of this world, the greatness of heaven,
the shortness of time, and the length of eternity."
Universal Prayer of Clement XI